Wedding Night
of a Nun

Wedding Night of a Nun

poems by

LYNNE LAWNER

An Atlantic Monthly Press Book

LITTLE, BROWN AND COMPANY · BOSTON · TORONTO

LIBRARY OF CONGRESS CATALOG CARD NO. 63-17423

FIRST EDITION

Some of these poems appeared in *Botteghe Oscure* and the
Atlantic Monthly. Acknowledgment is also due to Borestone
Mountain Poetry Awards (*Best Poems of 1955*) and to Random
House, Inc., for poems included in *Erotic Poetry,* edited by
William Cole.

ATLANTIC–LITTLE, BROWN BOOKS
ARE PUBLISHED BY
LITTLE, BROWN AND COMPANY
IN ASSOCIATION WITH
THE ATLANTIC MONTHLY PRESS

*Published simultaneously in Canada
by Little, Brown & Company (Canada) Limited*

PRINTED IN THE UNITED STATES OF AMERICA

Contents

[v]

Wedding Night
of a Nun

WEDDING NIGHT OF A NUN

Out of the flame of a glance
He delivered me.
Out of the rushing waters of the eye
Closing over my head,
The whip of the eyelash beating on the heart,
And the angled head,
From cool tortures of the slight movement
He delivered me.

From the oppression of the slender arm
And the cruel paradox of flesh —
White ways of midday
Full of shadow,
From the swift blade of a neck
Twisting tall and smooth
And the wilderness of a dark head,
He delivered me.

Yet I wonder as I lie with him tonight
And mumble praise into the vacant pillow,
If it is not the same
And he another, who, being what he is, has excuse
    for absence.
I see his form pass through the dark forest
And as I lie in terror and desire
Feel his breath upon my face
And my humanness.

[3]

WOMAN TO WOMAN

WOMAN to woman can cleave and crave,
But the restless heart and the aching bone
Beat for the meeting of sea and stone,
For woman to woman is wave upon wave.

As a pier that with the soft foam merges,
Harsh, then tender, men's needs move
Till strangeness shapes familiar love:
When turbulence ends, new life emerges.

No more, no more, sweet image, come,
Come trembling down to a still-water grave.
For woman to woman is wave upon wave
And breeds something pure, useless, and dumb.

PRAYER OF A YOUNG GIRL

O WHITE Diana,
You who spread the gauze
Twixt lover and lover
And catch up the blind hand
That moves over
Your sacred winding land,
You whose proud-faced law
Is steel to keep
And glass to break,
I would be a chaste Sicilian spring,
My waters sleeping, waking
With the movement of the tide,
A wild thing held by a silver string,
In deep woods hide
To watch the shadow of a torn stag
Stagger across the moon.

IN YOUR ARROGANCE

You think that when a woman yields
You own at least what you, harrowing, hurt.
But you cannot use my healing heart,
Though pared to a sickle, to cut down
What goldness grew when you were gone:
This is not your harvest, these are not your fields!

HIS LAMENT

WITHHELD, you were all mine, I knew,
Now you are love's. I would have kept you
As you left me, longing, not slept you
To death, to prove your living true.
Held at a distance, I could have you
With all the freedom that I gave you.
But now that you have come to stay,
I am grieved with going going away.

MAY SONG

WHAT wails from my womb
And undoomed drowns
Before thought of? Who crowns
This inch-king in a tomb
Of red seas, where no Moses
Decked with roses
Thorns his sweet way
To a quivering shore?
Each month I must say,
"A prophet I bore,
Who no more steals breath,"
I move towards my death.

FIX ME A BATCH OF BIRDS' TONGUES

Fix me a batch of birds' tongues
For I am an awkward speechless girl
In need of catching her breath
           that went out in a hot-kneed whirl
To warm his moon-nailed toes
     and caught its death
         of cold
             and froze.

From sparrows, swallows and wrens,
Finches and thrushes, rip
The little whip
And in my mouth set it fluttering,
So that the uttering
Of all those sought-for pains
Will seem less childish.

Before I grow old before I am young, I wish
Before I have told, or after,
How in his twisted ears he hung my heart
          from a cackling rafter,
To fix me a batch of birds' tongues
Learn my art.

DAPHNE

WHAT tunes on the casual wind
Will these ten shoots of leafy branches play
When night has raided every crevice? —
Shredded hair, stiff flesh
That felt the slightest flutter of air an invasion?
Though the sun plunders her,
Her lifted hands' gnarled knuckles
Hold off the sky,
A foot's fantastic flower
Resisting rain.
How did he wreak such changes,
His own body frail as a girl's?
Now hers, hardened to a tree's repetitive delicacies,
Suffers no human
Reproaches no god's touch.

A CHILD'S GARDEN

MOSTLY it was the furry leaves'
Ligustral pallor,
Scarlet of toxic berries
Among inextricable vines,
And the blue of bruised morning-glories
Opening as agonized mouth
Or other only half-known organ.

I suffered
Excruciating tortures of ants in peonies'
Florid pink folds, and always
Lilacs' trembling cones found their way into my
        mouth.
Stripped dandelions curled to taut spirals
In the excited water.

Tight knots of zinnias,
Fulvid tang at the nippled end
Of the soft season's
Curved tangent —
Nasturtiums.

FOR ALICIA, ON THE LOSS OF HER EYE

THE beauty was in having no reason riding to
    Venice.
Careening around a curve, the highway glaring at the
    moon,
Sleep seized him,
Machines went on of their own accord hurtling end
    over end.
When everything finally stopped,
The socket was like a gondola still softly rocking.

Now the surviving one, that would have fountained
    back lagoons,
Weeps for his forgetfulness and the blindness of the
    wheel,
The unconscious winding of the road
And the extinguishing of stars.

Where are the wings
for whom I made myself brittle
and portable,
one of a number of little glittering things
hawked
in the marketplace, talked
over by dirty boys
exchanging toys,

and scorned
sororities of chests, adorned
with golden chains,
and bellies that begged for legal pains,
naming me barren —
carrion
of a milked-silked generation
without veneration?

Where are the sliding feathers
for whom I shifted weathers:
the storms of continence
the deadly still-air of yielding,
the mental gelding,
the fleshly trance —
enduring any shit to shun
the domestic sun?

Since dung my dowry
I go in search of oxen, bulls,
instead of flowery
fools,
and like the Breton serf,
when he asked her,
I would rather sleep first
with my master.

Where are the claws and hooks
for whom all calms are crooks
robbing the rush
of anguish
that seeds the placid womb
and from the daily tomb
extracts steel epitaphs to blaze
in the urban haze?

And where is the beak that babbles
of the beautiful troubles
between men's legs
and moonward soarings of mythic stags,
and drowns out lovers' doting,
each word an abortion?
is savage chirping distortion,
is it better hating?

How low, how alien, how inconstant
must I grow to be played on,
to be preyed on
by your musical descent?
what horrors study,
what odd beds lie in,
to make a body
for a god to die in?

"TONGUE OF CRISP OLEANDER"

Tongue of crisp oleander, bole of green plane —
My mouth has never done anything but reach to-
    wards your pink tendrils,
My thighs but open peacefully to your grenade-hard
    seed.
You move through me as rifle-fire,
No recognizing rain,
Engendering destiny, desperation . . .
But we never touch.

"I WANT A MAN WHOSE USE CAN EXCEL"

I WANT a man whose use can excel
My most self-harming ingenuity,
Whose existence intrudes as a fruit into my hand,
Replete with difficulty.

Who, seeing buckets dip down a bottomless well
And every declared friend go thirsty,
Determines to squeeze the stonish fluid until a heart
Repents of impenetrability.

Where once I was a violent rock
That begged splitting, blindness, deception,
My form will curve like water in the vase
Of his warming perception.

FRAGMENTS OF A MEDITATION

I

Batted against our heads — every apricot stone,
Whether masonry pelting with centuried sucked-up
    sun
Or grapeseed flaunting new arbors on the tongue,
Our ardors are crushed, our cries the chance clang
Of one day's rusty armor struck from the wall,
Dead horses' hooves trampling our coupling — all
Pitted against us pitted against each other.

What woman would not throw her largest coin
Into that fountain? what man not passionately lean
Toward frescoed red-skinned dancers darkening?
Damp sanctuaries yawn — we in their reckless sleep
Dream dry spires of the instant, climb the clerestory,
    gape,
Then lose our watches, wills in airy cisterns,
Plugged into after-life — no candle burns.

II

      Forsythia
harder even than travertine,
lilacs and poppies overpowering,
hollyhock pollen stifling nostrils
in early summer stillness, bees
burning my mouth before boys;
already corn kernels cowed me,
buckeyes made me slip, so
sleek they lay with their
little recurring scars, I
with my growing single one —
I didn't need this aqueduct-dry
plain, Tarquinian wild bleached wheat
mocking the vermilion flesh in the cave.

III

When you sailed to me in unironed sheets billowed
with sun, flapped from rooftops over where we har-
    bored
in light from the storms of colder continents,
we were as native as our songs, my arms
trellised your head.
Mayflower was now October oakleaf crumpling in the
    fire
of return — we were without war, with only the ex-
    cruciating pain of our own unfolding corollas,
    corollaries.
We woke to the beating of rugs and thought of Africa,
not the beating of backs, but of tambours for our
    pleasure.

Oblique guilt — could we stun it in piazza glare,
reflect it back to gas-stained fingers,
wash it out as Tivoli's women wash bloody cloths each
    month (so many nostrils unbreathed into) and
    as cypress gardens are washed by a myriad of
    fountains?
No! — neither brute simplicity nor aesthetic ecstasy,
it faced us on red walls at every turning, and we be-
    came the fiery shame of which these were the
    ashes.

IN THE BORGHESE ZOO

THROUGH the blond trees his haze of hair,
Her fierce discretion.
Flushed flamingoes and lavender gazelles
The acme of passion.
"Yes," I say to your occult question:
"Do captive lions make love?"
(But why do these two go dressed in black
Beneath the olive?)

CIPRIANA

A THOUSAND re-kindlings
And *Pauline* in a lunar stupor,
Repelling the beating lashes
Of loves far too impure.

As all of spangled Rome
Gives up its daily shine,
In the dark sky of your pupils
Cupolas spill their red wine.

A COMPASSION LIKE CATHERINE'S

NICOTINE, orange blossom —
All day long I'm haunted by your taste
Through squalid passages of urban viscera.

If the exquisite Sienese saint said,
"His wounded side is a perfume shop
Binding me to my vow,"

Imagine what rash promises your mouth's
Aura of smoke and bergamot
Extorts from my heart.

Remember how, pain
And the city shut off,
Your odorous solitude lay in my warm hand?

PUGLIA

OLIVES in twisted colloquy, the lowering storm,
Broom-swept rock half-lucent as smoked glass
Watch with calm the struck Vespa smash
Legs, chrome crush the burrowing worm.

A quaint stone wall: we haul him, howling, from the road
To the local unstaffed hospital where the white
Sister Superior with her two canaries sits out
Easter, disaster, and the astral sinking of the toad.

Your eyelids' fluttering silhouette
against purple dawn
tells how your sleep yet divides
me
from a dream
of me.

I watch
dahlias jag open,
liquid too viscous for tears
coat green stamen
bunched in a Prussian
bull's-eye;

hear
rustle of outer petal,
light thunder, words,
"Let me breathe
what you reject,"
stir slumber;

know
I will grow into your dream of me,
real as the rain we wake to
when dark lashes, dissembling
sleep, tremble with
recognition, part.

[25]

CONTINGENCIES

WINDOWS spangled with sun
And all the air a great unfolding rose.
Tracery of trees on stone,
Debris on water.

Lost in deceptive spaces of contingencies
My hair turns chestnut,
Burns,
Smoking in the early evening of your eyes.

I saw her shoot
that boyhood down —
a hot quail's bronze
late-summer flight —
shyness too swollen for humility,
thought uncautious of a huntress' advent,
stupefied to a brilliant detachment —
ruffled, untender, precocious;

saw that foot
hooked on terse air
cleave to purity, claw azure,
watched blood immerse the sandstone ring
of impermeable neck, heard crack of rifle
after still echo
in that furry ear
pitched to the chime of titmouse hunger;

saw him rise flaming,
nearly obscene with new-found passion,
all his hues smoldering
in her cool fixed gaze,
fall to the circling altar beyond catcher and caught,
craving what made both
prey
to all-devouring Autumn.

ALÉXANDRINE

WE needed to go south that year.
Commerce of petals and arms pale with talc
Already beckoned our departure.
The scented tangle we made
Decried the city's discus-throw into September.
The new bikini kindled an immodest spring,
And on the slow train south
Our entwined hands made steeples tropical.

When from the beach we saw her
In her tarzan chintz
Huge negroid rising
From the sea's white riffled
Reconciliation with chill winds —
The feline smile above the Buddhist flanks,
Flesh seeming to push brocade seemed
To hold us in its ambiguous warmth.

Through moonless fronds
And laurel-roses' half-imagined smell,
Our love imperfect because, undetached,
One still moved towards the other,
She hurled her immobile jungle
Zero in our tentative path.
And we found the south, found each other's mouth
Hanging from her big black teats.

POSSESSION

Each time his will abdicated,
The undisputed acreage
Of what he owned of me
Grew,
And mere blond hair rose shocks of corn
To his electric gaze.
Soft shifts in sleep
So as not to wake me with the rudeness
Of his restless dreaming of me told me
What did I want more than his saying,
"Let me do what you want"?
Often at dawn I found him
Poised leanly above me,
Jealous of light and of sea air,
Not daring to touch.
And all that time a body
Was signing away lands, stocks, estates,
To turn over to him,
Over and over.
I'd come a long way for someone scared to trust.

RECOGNITION

My nails are weighted with transparency.
Though you touch each luminous mute syllable,
I know I am not anything you can name.
Surfaces flicker in your fist,
Glow, being irretrievable.

Each week I blow out rows of wax prisons.
Then in the darkness there's your ear's definition
And your pupil's defiance, there's the art
Of your tenderness after and candor before
Each fresh annihilation . . .

. . . from which I surge pinpointed, exalted, eccen-
tric,
Knowing I am not anything you can name.
If something precise and painful in your gaze
Catches at fugitive cinders, clasps
Flame within flame,

It's yours — all the hurt which you recognize.

NIGHTINGALES AT NEMI

NIGHTINGALES at Nemi
Dark chirps of pebbles echo,
Dove flocks reverse on water,
Silver chips.

Where flushed young bougainvillea
Thickens to purple,
Dian, the heavy-with-child's hope and virgin's,
Walks,

Strews strawberries, oaks, and violets
On a bridal sheet
The almost black lake mirrors, marries
Rich terraces to a gaping crater.

CHESTNUTS

WILD chestnuts weep,
The grief of their oblong leaves more brilliant
Than all sullen shimmering of fir.
He blows on her fingers as an oboe introspects,
Darkening woods so there's no more season.
Fear and the bosky dropping of progression —
This standstill tremor
Invades each needle until, resinous with tension,
It pleads for semblances of change.

"Stay back," crackle invidious oaks
At the base of whose wracked henna
Ancient ferns, worn out with heritage,
Oscillate in mid-yellows.
Each note clinches her into endurance,
Mutes natural cries to be killed,
As almond eyes through ravaged groves
Make opaque dumb
Thickets of disbelief in greenness.

Edging a black lake herons
Perilously step,
Words touch seclusion, withdraw.
In the hollow of trust, no raven-warnings,
No nestless murmurings of dried trees,
Only chestnuts' rhythmical bleeding
Into calmed air, terror:
"What if his breath goes, and I thrive
Alone, unconsoled by savage autumn?"

Do not come, contentment,
To shackle me with ease,
Who would laugh so at the words:
"This lady is for burning."
Although the bed teems with ashes,
Behind the still lashes of my love's eyes
New desire kindles.

Do not come, contentment.
Serenity long precedes you,
Waging her cool war in my blood.
Surely she'll not forsake me now if I wish
Respite from living,
When, with his arms too hotly screwed about my
    neck, I crave
Brief gray Athenian lapses.

GOOD GIRL

To live long with such violence is to make
Placid loopholes of oneself, to hope
Escape through the air of standing still.

And she will go on hanging herself with the rope
Of practiced stupor before her father, until
Another man's touch jars her into earthquake.

THE COME-BACK

THAT blighted bilious past
Reflected in the chartreuse swimming
Of this drowned sumac's
Slats quavering beyond venetians
Slaps her in the face, reminds,
Repeats its damage. Those few phalli
Flocked to, swiftly shunned
And turned away from, follow still
With little accusing momentary
Hurts. She was a bitch, yes,
But in the long run violable
And stable, able to give
Exactly what was ruefully suspected
Later. Tart grapes: in her confused
And unrelated summer came each
Bearing a story of subsequent heartache
That made her look hard
Down corridors of compromise, divorce, worse —
Strange marriages and stiff conformities.
And she, full of a guilty half-assed
Will to right wrongs, sample perhaps
Fruit long since elsewhere apportioned,

Feel what she missed, passed time
One at a time with them in slow
Slightly unsure gropings towards tentative
Touchings on sore spots and new tenderness.
But how to recover
Shipwrecked fragments in the leaves,
Half-submerged in foliage, lost?
This dream of health hid
Cessation of growth and death of parts,
Limbs hacking themselves off,
Veins' sallow swell into a kind of cobweb
Malignancy. There was no use trying.
One thing had, the other
Would still elude them.
No practiced freshness could half fulfill
What then was wanted; interim loyalties
Felled her slim hopes of stirring up some
Sudden burgeoning
Of former awkward gestures towards attachment.
No atonement, no rearrangement,
Just old quirks and fears and mutual
Shuttings-off. Mature, if unwise, worldly,
They found — she in a new softness,
They in a new search for softness —
No way to stop happening old hurts, hates,
As blinds closed tight. Sweltering
In interiors, forced to recall how once
She denied greenness, she wonders
What's become of between-times
Beauty — slopes scarcely left, those gentler

Hands. She pulls a dress herself
Over her head, that comes off smoothly.
Some bruises. But the thin waves
Wafted from trees down windows
Wash through the pits of her arms,
All other hollows, in the light —
Bridges, far-off ships.
Somewhere fair arbors
Are anchored in this autumn, yearning
Answered, vestiges of known things
Fused with new. Nothing
Forgiven for everything given.
(He will be returning, too.)

HOSPITALITY

Guest in my body,
Your host respects old laws:
Nothing you ask for can be refused,
Neither the flaws

Of a vase that is your quest
And treasure, nor the long dream,
Excluding you, of abstract pleasures
Impregnable seam.

For you the gift not made yet
Rises as from a vault.
But will it, shaped to your imagined need,
Be without fault?

BEING angry with him is like an absence in me.
Hart-shooting hunter who finds he was the most
    beautiful,
In my mind I try to resurrect that slim rabbity
    shape —
White belly smoothed down from a small waist,
Pained expressions, timidity,
Eyes imploring me at last to be peaceful.

The hurt in the chest is a lack, not a presence —
Intangible reaching that strains muscles, makes the
    heart
Hammer as if striving to hide the want of his,
The ear turn where a voice once was.
His slightest eccentric gesture was my whole balance.
I go to pieces now with the vain effort.

When the will exiles yet desires, it is like an axe
Felling its own timber, hewing its own sharp edge:
There is the smell of heated metal —
Futile reminder of a man's sweat.
His distance is a sickness no amputation can fix,
No patience alter, and no weight of anguish assuage.

SHADE

INDOORS our world was shade,
The sumac
Refracted watery
Through windows off a dark shaft,
Nerves end to end
Contracted in the dimness of their own
Reflexes.
Light from the wall of the next building
Fell through venetians
Onto his thighs forking the bed —
Trick sofa now swallowing the room.
Later, his asleep form
Seemed to collect
Even the half-blond hair-ends
Crackling
Towards his outstretched fingers in vague profusion.

MEETING THE FAMILY

Ten Carolina days, all my warming,
I refused, thinking to be safe
Away from people who might claim me
As she who made their son awaken
In the night crying, "Where has she gone?"

With my own words in the north
I made a noose of corn tassels,
Stood outside in the chill wind dreaming
Of tall forms moving through tobacco
And was a ghost everywhere.

DANAË

No one was ever richer than I,
Even whose waste is fecund;
In my feces are golden glints
Like eyes assaying through brown irises
My half-bleached hair streaming from the end of summer.

IN THE MARSH

In the marsh like me I saw
Mallow out of the noxious dregs rising —
Inkling of mauve against sky-yellow,
Dark reeds, burnt crackers pollen-fused.

Nearby were ferns, rampant grapevines,
Their small sour green nipples sagging.
In scum lily pads jostled, roots surged
Tangling at the sallow surface.

Rushes not up to cane-size, colorless,
Wild blossoms beaded, powdery,
Queen Anne's lace — fresh surfeit
Skirting the night's thick still-water edge.

In the marsh like me, fallow, I saw
Masked in queer beauty, light-shedding,
Loosestrife, violet, scattered on tall stems,
Everything to its knees in anxious bracken.